STAGED!

A Four-Step Process to Stand Out in Your Personal and Professional Life

Conrod S. J. Kelly

Thank you for your
Support! I hope this
Books gives you the
courage to STEP UP
&
STAND
OUT,

STAGES

— Step up - Stand out —

DEDICATION

Lighting The Fire

This book is dedicated to those who sparked a light in me and gave me the courage to shine bright for the world to see.

CONTENTS

ACKNOWLEDGMENTS

I would first like to thank my Lord and Savior Jesus Christ for giving me my talents so that I may share them with the world.

I would like to thank my parents, Michael and Florence Kelly, for bringing me into this world and teaching me the principles I live by, which have allowed me to achieve all that I have thus far.

I would like to thank my little brother and sister, Travis and Michaela, whose entrance into this world made me a brother and role model.

I would like to thank my wife, friend, and life partner Joy, who has supported me on this journey.

I want to thank my friends and family who over the years have supported me no matter what the circumstance. I want to specifically acknowledge April, Armond, Bassy, Bernadette, Bianca, Damien, Darrell, David, Delisha, Ernie, Guiselle, Kamal, Kris, Lee, Melissa, Olisa, Regine, Renita, Ronita, Shanel, Sheltoine, Sherry, Tarrah, Terrence, Yael, and Yolanda.

I want to thank my advisors, mentors and sponsors who always told me the truth, whether I wanted to hear it or not. Specifically I would like to thank Charlotte, Cleveland, Deb, Deborah, Erica, Eric, Erik, Eunice, James, Joseph, Lisa Caldwell, Lisa Callahan, Lori, Marjorie, Michele, Nina, Tom, and Tricia.

I want to thank my business coach and friend Sonia who has held my hand through the process of becoming an entrepreneur and author.

I want to thank Clarence Armbrister for introducing me to the concept of "setting myself on fire."

I want to thank my Executive Leadership Council Bright Futures class and instructors for holding me accountable. I told you I would not let you all down.

I want to thank my previous and current employer and coworkers. They have been the biggest supporters of my passion and my purpose.

I want to thank the following women who changed my trajectory because of their words, vision, actions, love, and support.

Mrs. Juanita Albury—For recognizing my gift

Ms. Thelma White Horton—For making me mentally tough

Mrs. Kathleen Hoffman—For challenging me to be better than good enough

Mrs. Josephine Stinson—For taking a chance on me

Dr. Sybil Mobley—For having the vision to create a program that accepted nothing less than excellence

Ms. Jane Quinn—For giving me additional time to learn. Who knew that all I had to do was ask for it?

Lastly, I want to acknowledge the moment that changed my life forever. The day when my mother quit her job to watch her eleven-year-old son give a five-minute speech at a peer mediators conference because she believed that much in him and what he was capable of becoming. It is a debt that I hope to never repay because it fuels my determination every day.

FOREWORD

When I first began my career in the Pharmaceutical Industry more than twenty-five years ago, I could have used a book like *STAGED!* There were many books on the market that taught me how to dress, how to speak and how to "go along to get along." But I needed more. At a time when there were few role models with whom I could personally identify, I consumed every book I could find. Still, what was missing were books that encouraged me to own my career development, clarify my goals, establish a personal brand and celebrate my authentic self.

Despite the fact that there were very few role models, I did successfully climb the corporate ladder. I now have a seat at a number of decision-making tables, both at work and in the global community. While the **journey** was not always simple or what I expected, what I know for sure is that it was made a little easier with a network of individuals who supported, encouraged and generally "had my back" along the way. They helped me to effectively tackle issues everyone faces in the workplace, such as getting promoted faster and making a bigger impact. They also provided much-needed perspective so that I did not lose sight of the things in life that are truly important.

STAGED! will take you on a similar journey of self-discovery by giving you the tools to uncover your strengths, understand your opportunities, establish your personal brand, and embrace your story.

I have known Conrod Kelly for many years, first as an MBA recruit (the one that got away!) and later as a rising talent at Merck & Co., Inc. (we got him back!). He is a lifelong learner, constantly building his knowledge base. He is a highly creative thinker who consistently seeks new ways to add value. He is a teacher who provides compelling lessons on how to gain a competitive edge in a tough business environment. But most of all, he is a leader who always inspires others to do their best work. I am grateful our paths have crossed.

I urge you to read *STAGED!* with pen in hand. Take time to honor the process and reflect on the questions; be thoughtful about your responses. What will emerge is a plan to help you become your Best Self. Once you have been "Staged", you will have the knowledge you need to take control of your career and build a life in which you are the "writer, producer and lead actor."

STAGED! allows you to explore, reflect and - most importantly - Dream Big.

The power to transform your career and your life is closer than you think. *STAGED!* will show you how!

Charlotte O. McKines
Vice President, Global Marketing
Merck & Co., Inc.

HABIT

I am your constant companion.

I am your greatest helper or heaviest burden.

I will push you onward or drag you down to failure. I am completely at your command.

Half of the things you do, you might as well turn over to me and I will do them—quickly and correctly.

I am easily managed—you must be firm with me. Show me exactly how you want something done and after a few lessons, I will do it automatically.

I am the servant of great people, and alas, of all failures as well. Those who are great, I have made great. Those who are failures, I have made failures. I am not a machine though I work with the precision of a machine plus the intelligence of a person.

You may run me for profit or run me for ruin—it makes no difference to me.

Take me, train me, be firm with me, and I will place the world at your feet.

Be easy with me and I will destroy you.

Who am I? I am Habit.

—Unknown

1

TO MASTER IT, TEACH IT

One of the things I believe has contributed to my success is the fact that the foundation of my education was built on the principle of learning by doing and teaching. In my business school, every student was a teacher and every teacher a student. The dean of my business school, Dr. Sybil Mobley, believed that the best way to get people to learn was to put them in environments to demonstrate an understanding of the material and then reinforce the learning by having them teach it to others. Throughout my matriculation at Florida A & M University's School of Business and Industry, this symbiotic approach deepened my understanding of the content, created a bond between schoolmates, and immersed me in a culture of continuous learning. The repetitive action of acquiring knowledge, putting it into practice, and then sharing it with others became a habit that ultimately formed the basis of my character.

While I know verbal contracts can be difficult to enforce, in order to get the most out of this book I am asking you to commit to doing two things:

1) Try to apply what you learn each and every day.

2) Teach others what you learn or discover as a result of reading this book.

Now that I have your commitment, I'd like to introduce you to my recommended approach for reading this book. The reason I am being so prescriptive is because good habits do not happen by accident. They require purpose, process, preparation, practice, persistence, and patience.

1) Read the chapter.

2) Take a couple of days to reflect on what you have read.

3) Tell someone about what you have learned.

4) Make a commitment to apply what you have learned.

5) Ask someone to hold you accountable.

6) Share your progress with someone you trust.

I particularly want to emphasize steps two and four, which are deeply rooted in two essential beliefs that I have. The first is that thought should always precede action and second, your actions are the foundation of your habits.

Practice

If you want to develop good habits, you must embrace the act of practice. You have to be both purposeful and persistent in your practice. Nothing has or can be achieved without practice. The more you practice, the more things will come to you naturally. It becomes unconscious competence. It becomes your character and your destiny. My only word of caution is that you must also be patient with yourself and accept that it is a process. Be sure to take time to celebrate the small wins along the journey. As I mentioned previously, the repetitive action of acquiring knowledge, putting it into practice, and then sharing it with others is a habit of mine. To demonstrate this, I have infused "Real World, Real Things Moments" throughout the book to share with you what I have learned on my journey.

2

INCEPTION

Take a few minutes to reflect on the word inception.

How would you explain it to someone?

What words would you say are synonymous with inception?

Did you come up with any of the following?

Birth, Origin, Start,

Begin, Source, Dawn,

Outset, Launch, Root,

Genesis, Kick-off, Emergence

When I look at this list of words holistically, a few themes emerge. The first theme centers on how things come to be. Understanding the how and or why gives people a sense of purpose. Even when there may not be evidence of the how or why, the absence of proof is often the source of incredible strength, sometimes referred to as faith. The second theme focuses on the commencement of a journey. Inherent in any word describing the beginning of something is a level of energy that is fueled by thoughts of what awaits at the final destination—or the uncertainty of what will be experienced along the way. Depending on your personality, this energy can be the source of gravity-defying inspiration or fear that renders you immobile. The choice, the final theme, is yours on how to use this energy. Nothing in this world is more powerful than choice. Faith is a choice. Starting a process is a choice. Our lives are directed by the choices we make or fail to make.

So what exactly is inception? Merriam Webster dictionary defines it as an act, process, or instance of beginning. If you are a movie aficionado like me, you may have thought of Christopher Nolan's 2010 movie, *Inception*. Without providing a full synopsis of the movie, the story line revolves around a group of individuals attempting to plant an idea in the mind of the target while they are dreaming. The movie reveals that an idea can be a powerful, yet manipulative force. Used appropriately, an idea can unlock the unimaginable. Used incorrectly, it can lead people to do the unthinkable.

During the film, several key characters are introduced who play an important role in embedding an idea inside the mind of the target. The extractor was someone who knew how to influence the target to reveal his or her deepest thoughts. The architect designed the dream, which the extractor would bring the target into. The architect did not provide all of the details for the dream world; the target's projections, details from their own subconscious and memories, filled in any blanks. By having the target fill in all the details, it convinced them that the world built by the architect was real.

The Real World

Is it just me or do dreams feel real while we are in them? When I think of some of my more memorable dreams, it was only when I woke up that I felt like something was strange. In my opinion, dreams are often projections of a culmination of ideas you have been exposed to or your own ideas. Good or bad, have you ever done or said things in your dreams that you could never bring yourself to do in reality? Did the joy or pain associated with your actions feel real? When we are in a deep state of dreaming, the dream can feel so real that the mind stops trying to wake up and accepts the dream as reality.

What do you dream about? List out as many ideas as you can come up with.

Take the time to mark this page so that you can refer back to it.

My dreams feel so real at times that I occasionally wake up drenched in sweat, breathing intensely, or even crying because of how real the emotions felt. I am not even sure if it is possible, but sometimes I wake up in the middle of a dream, fall back asleep, and pick up where the dream left off. This may seem strange to you, but I feel like the writer, director, and lead actor in my dreams. My dreams give me the feeling that I can control my own dreams.

Real World, Real Things Moment
Write, Direct, and Star in Your Career Development

One of the biggest misconceptions people have about their career and professional development is that it is the responsibility of someone else. I wish I had a dollar for every time I heard "my manager didn't develop me." It is true that both your manager and company plays a role in your development, but you own the lion share. There are three ways that you can develop yourself. This can happen by doing, learning on your own or through others. Seek out a leadership role in your company's employee resource group, your church, or a community service organization that will allow you to refine or develop new skill sets. Continuous learning is a major pillar for career development. Subscribe to industry-specific journals, newsletters, or blogs; attend conferences or networking events for your field; or take an online course to freshen up on old concepts or learn new ones. Last, develop and tap into your network by securing a mentor, coach, and sponsor. These individuals can help you choose where you want to go, when you should go, who needs to know, and what you need to do to be ready when an opportunity presents itself. This is a long way of saying you have to be the writer, director, and lead actor in pursuing your career goals.

Dream Big

How often have you heard the phrase dream big? Intrinsic in that statement is the idea that you are able to control your own dreams. Your dreams do not have to be confined to sleep or a departure from reality. Your dreams are the visionary manifestation of the ideas and goals that will guide you from your current reality to your desired reality. Many of us have goals or dreams that we have put on the back burner or have decided to no longer pursue. It is my intent to help encourage you to not let go of those dreams by giving you a process to follow.

GPS

One of the most famous dreams is memorialized in Martin Luther King's "I Have a Dream" speech. His dream inspired a nation and will continue to influence generations to come. His dream was a roadmap for how we as a nation could travel from our current reality to a place where all men are created equal. Within his speech he laid out several goals for the country. What I love about goals is that they are mile markers in life that let you know whether you are making progress or you are going in the wrong direction. Goals remind me that the road to success is paved with small wins. Many speculate that Dr. King knew he would not live to see his dream fully realized, but it was with his faith, the substance of things hoped for and evidence of things not seen, that allowed him to keep pursuing the impossible dream.

I am going to go out on a limb and assume that most of you have dared to dream; you have even dared to dream big. I'm referring to living out your dreams and not confining them to the few hours that you are asleep at night. I too am a dreamer, and I am inviting you inside of my dream world where everyone has the opportunity to become whatever it is they desire, if they are willing to step up and stand out.

Dream House

One of things people often dream about is their dream house. I want you to go back to the list of things you dream about and pick one. I now want you to imagine that the dream you have selected will now become your dream home. I will be your architect for this project, but I will only create a frame for the home. It will be up to you to leverage your ideas and experiences to make this house a home. There is not unlimited space in this home so you will have to choose carefully what elements you will carry over from your past to make sure there is room for the future. My goal is to extract those ideas and experiences that will make your dreams a reality by shepherding you through a process as my mother did for me.

Real World, Real Things Moment
Manipulation Through Inspiration

Since my inception, no one has been more methodical at planting ideas in my head than my mother. I have now come to realize that my five-foot-two mother, with her big smile and even bigger heart, may be the most manipulative

CONROD S. J. KELLY

person in my life, and I am so grateful for it. My mother always had words of inspiration for me like:

- Doing just the homework that what was assigned means everyone is on the same page. Going ahead gives you an advantage.

- Practice it until you can do it without thinking.

- Bad practice will get you bad results. Excellent practice will get you excellent results.

- Always be on your best behavior, because you never know who is watching you.

Genius

"Genius is one percent inspiration and ninety-nine percent perspirations."—Thomas Edison

The best example of my mother's manipulation was her referring to me as her little genius. Sure mothers are proud of their kids, but who goes around calling their child a genius before they have even taken an I.Q. test? Only as an adult have I come to realize how wise my mother was. By referring to me as a genius, she helped me develop my self-esteem and confidence at an early age. Additionally, because I believed that I was a "genius," I worked my butt off to make sure my grades reflected my genius status. When I came across the quote above, it all seemed to make sense.

Many of you may have experienced the type of inception that I did. It could have come in the form of a parent, teacher, manager, or mentor. The ideas that were planted may have helped to define you in a positive manner or set you on a negative course. It is my intent to perform "inception" on you to support your pursuit of a new goal or getting you back on the right track. To make this dream a reality, a plan and a deadline is required, and through the staging process, I will help you come up with one.

What is your "inception" story?

3

HOME STAGING

One Big Movie Set

One of the fastest growing trends in real estate is the use of home staging. Some of you may be familiar with home staging, and for others it may be a new concept. We live in a world that is so driven by staging that we do not even notice it because it is the norm. Neighborhoods, malls, department stores, car showrooms, grocery stores, and hotels are laid out in a specific way to focus your attention on what they want you to see, how they want you to see it and when they want you to see it. Yes, they are staged! Similar to the dream world in the movie *Inception*, it is you who projects your thoughts, emotions, and memories into these environments that drive your decisions and behaviors.

Be Intentional

Throughout this book, I am going to focus on the principles of home staging that you can apply to pursuing your dream, or as stated earlier, completing that dream home. The most common criticism about home staging and what you may also say about this book is that it is common sense. Much of what you're going to learn from this book may sound perfectly obvious, and you might have done it even without me recommending it. My goal is to reinforce and encourage you to do things intentionally and not by chance. My friend Shelley would always remind me to be intentional about my goals and not allow things to happen just by chance. She would always reinforce that I was in control because I had the ability to choose. Whenever I would try to give luck the credit for any of my accomplishments, my best friend Darrell would remind me of Seneca Roman's quote, "Luck is what happens when preparation meets opportunity." I choose to be prepared which is why I am so "lucky."

Competitive Advantage

At its core, home staging is about gaining a competitive advantage over similar homes in the area. In more simplistic terms, it comes down to determining what or who your competition is and what makes you better. While it may be easy to identify the natural competitor, take into consideration the fact that doubt, fear, anger, bad habits, complacency, and a lack of preparation can be competitors as well. Sometimes the choices we make or the things we tell ourselves, make us our own fiercest competitors.

Refer back to the dream you selected earlier in the book.

What is your competitive advantage?

What makes you best suited to accomplish your dream?

Who or what is your competition?

Who or what could get in the way of you achieving your dream?

Home staging involves accentuating the home's advantages and eliminating or reducing perceived negatives. Staging focuses on using marketing to shape how buyers perceive your home and its features. When staging a home, the intent should not be to hone into your own particular taste, or comfort zone, but to focus on the buyer who will be attracted to your house.

What have you done to accentuate your advantages and eliminate or reduce your perceived weaknesses?

Who knows about your dreams?

What do they think about them?

This is probably the best opportunity to let you know that you may end up being the buyer of your own home. Some people are living in a home they own with a renter's mindset. After taking the steps to stage a home, many people often change their mind about selling it. Let me explain.

Real World, Real Things Moment
Renting Versus Buying Your Goals

I have a theory that there are a lot of people in this world who rent their goals. Many of us grew up with rented goals from our parents, teachers, or even our mentors. Think about the last time you rented a car or even stayed in a hotel room. Did you wash, wax, and vacuum your rental car? Did you make up the bed and clean the bathroom in your hotel room? When you rent things, you depend on the person who owns it to do the maintenance. When you own it, it is up to you, even if you have to pay someone to help you. It is great that we inherit goals that give us direction and purpose, but there will come a time when you have to decide if they are still the right goals for you. The staging process and principles give you the opportunity to reshape your perspectives—an opportunity to reshape how you see yourself and how others see you. Once again, this process will require patience. I am still trying to figure out how to own my brand by bringing how people see me, how I see myself, and how I want to be seen into alignment.

Change Creates Change ($)

Taking the time to stage a home can pay off big. Complete renovations are rarely needed, but there will certainly be some essential changes. By choosing to stage a home, it's very possible to have a quicker sale and larger return. Many real estate agents will list a home only if it has been staged because they know how much easier and more profitable the transaction will be if the investment—of time, effort, and a little money—has been made. By staging, all the work for potential buyers has already been done—they do not have to imagine the home's potential. The necessary preparations were already taken to show the home at its best.

Real World, Real Things Moment
I Make Myself So Easy to Sell

Landing a job, building your network, or securing funding to start a business, often requires having someone "vouch" or "sponsor" you. Just like how a real estate agent may not want to work with a home that has not been staged, someone may be hesitant to advocate on your behalf for a promotion, introduce you to someone in their network, or form a relationship with you if they feel that you haven't made the necessary investments in yourself.

A Staging Mindset

Rather than staging your home only when it is necessary, it is my hope that you will take on a staging mentality. A staging mentality is built on purpose, process, preparation, practice, persistence, and patience. Let it be your new way of thinking and behaving. I strongly believe that once you make the choice to do so, it will become a backdrop to all that you do—a habit that will create fantastic life results and shape your destiny. It is the choices we make that change our circumstances. Believe it or not, seemingly small changes can make a tremendous difference. However, just because something may seem small does not mean that it requires a small amount of effort. Often times I feel people work harder to avoid the extra effort than to actually apply the effort that will produce the originally desired outcome.

Return on Investment

According to a survey conducted by Homegain.com, people who spent $500 on staging recovered over 343 percent of the cost when they sold their home. Imagine the returns you could achieve by investing in yourself: taking an online course, learning a new skill, or taking a class on public speaking. The idea behind following the staging process and adopting it as way of thinking is that exponential rewards can be achieved if additional effort is put towards achieving your goals and it is done in the proper sequence.

By taking you through each step of the staging process, it is my intention to help you become more self-aware. Becoming self-aware is an exercise in discovering, accepting, and acting upon the truth. When you are self-aware, you can be honest about who you are and what you want: two critical pieces of information for achieving your professional and personal goals. If you decide to go through this process, along the way you will be presented with a choice to act upon what you have learned. If you choose not to, then you are the owner of the outcomes associated with not taking action. You must be willing to do the work to achieve your desired results.

There are four key principles that I have discovered in home staging:

1. Do your homework.

2. Declutter, clean, and repair.

3. Ensure there is curb appeal.

4. Tell your home's story.

In order for this process to work for you, you have to commit to a few things.

1) Remember your purpose.

2) Respect and embrace the process.

3) Take time to prepare for each new step.

4) Commit to practicing.

5) Be persistent in your pursuit.

6) Adopt patience with yourself and others.

Persistence is extremely important in this process because you never know when opportunity will knock. Remember, the choices you make today will enable you to control your destiny or will put your destiny firmly in the hands of others.

So let's take the first step by doing some homework!

4

HOMEWORK

Oh Snap!

The first step in the home-staging process requires taking a step back to look at a home through the eyes of a buyer. One of the best ways to accomplish this is through photographs. Photographs have a unique ability to capture what the eye does not see. They reveal exactly what a home looks like to outsiders, which aids in identifying the changes that need to be made to a home. Until one sees that there is room for improvement, there is no reason to proceed. Similarly, one cannot fix a problem they do not know exists.

Roses

There is an old saying that an arrogant person walks around as if their "stuff" doesn't smell. Outkast, the Atlanta based rap duo, profited from this saying with their hit song "Roses." So you may be wondering why I am bringing this up. Passing the sniff test is a huge part of home staging as well as becoming more self-aware. When it comes to home staging, most people make the mistake of trying to cover up the smells rather than take care of the source. It amazes me how hard people will work to avoid the extra effort required to permanently address the issue. People will spend hundreds on air fresheners, candles, plug-ins, or Arm & Hammer instead of throwing away old food, fixing a leak, or taking out the trash. No matter how large, exquisite, or updated a home is, if it has an unpleasant odor, it will be much harder to sell. Every home has a scent, but unless the owner gets feedback from someone who doesn't live in it, they'll never know whether it's a deterrent to someone buying it.

Real World, Real Things Moment
The Sniff Test

Now while having good hygiene and a home that doesn't smell is important, the sniff test is a metaphor for getting an outsiders opinion. When you get so close or attached to who you are or who you think you are, sometimes referred to as the ego, it is often difficult to see your blind spots. Most of us have aspects of our traits that are obvious to everyone but ourselves. Ask a friend, a mentor, or a co-worker who doesn't spend much time with you to give you a sniff.

"I See," Said the Blind Man.

The range of what we think and do is limited by what we fail to notice. And because we fail to notice that we fail to notice, there is little we can do to change: until we notice how failing to notice shapes our thoughts and deeds.—R.D. Laing

Blinds spots can be hard to find because they are often buried in denial. Denial is a refusal to believe in something or admit that something exists. There is also an inability to recognize or unwillingness to deal with the proverbial elephant in the room. This is often rooted in the sometimes unpleasant nature of the truth and the perception that feedback is accusatory. Denial is a close relative of fear, which functions to protect the ego and requires a substantial investment of energy.

Redirecting that energy to search for your blind spots can be a difficult undertaking, but it can lead to a transcendent accomplishment. Identifying your own blind spots is an exercise in contradiction, because if you can see them, they are no longer blind to you. So how do you find your blind spots? Blind spots are repetitive experiences that make you question why something always happens to you. For example: you keep ending up in jobs you hate, you always have a terrible boss, you always have "bad luck," or people consistently perceive you differently than you see yourself. If the evidence suggests that you have blind spots, you can try to eliminate them by first asking yourself, "Why am I afraid to see what is really happening?" Fear is the archenemy of acceptance, which allows you to recognize and acknowledge what is actually happening.

While tackling your fears may lead to some meaningful insights, the more efficient approach may be soliciting feedback from others. I would recommend starting with someone closest to you and then branching out. Astonishingly, relative strangers are often the best resources for feedback. Even though I know how valuable honest feedback can be, I still have to force myself to ask for it. Any form of feedback is scary, but the kind that tackles your blind spots can be unbearable. That's why, before you ask for honest feedback, you should have a strategy in place. Fortunately for you, I have a strategy you can use.

The best tool you have for handling solicited feedback is choice. You can choose the date, time, location, length, topics, objectives, and so on. In order for the feedback session to be meaningful, you have to be in a place where you are open to receiving it. Now that we have that out of the way, here are some other tips you can use while receiving feedback.

1. Consider the source and their intent.

2. Listen actively to what is being said and how it is being said.

3. Summarize what you hear to confirm you are interpreting it correctly.

4. Ask clarifying questions.

5. Focus on the facts and not opinions.

6. Identify one or two things you agree with that you can act on and put a plan in place.

Appraisal

The homework process in home staging requires finding out what features that competing homes possess, what condition they are in, and what the asking prices are. Knowing this information is important in helping decide how much time and money to spend to invest in staging a home. It will also helps in assessing where the competition may be vulnerable. In real estate, this is sometimes referred to as an appraisal. One of the best resources for getting a hold of this information is a real estate agent or an appraiser.

Real World, Real Things Moment
Managing Expectations

Getting an "appraisal" is a critical component of the job-search process. Throughout my years in corporate America, I have always volunteered to assist with recruiting efforts. While it is rewarding to help shape someone's career and build the talent pool for the organization, it can be frustrating to see the lack of preparation by potential candidates. This lack of preparation normally materializes as misalignment between the role they are applying for, their qualifications, and their salary expectations. There are tons of websites out there, such as salary.com, vault.com, and glassdoor.com that can help candidates manage salary expectations. Company job boards and websites like LinkedIn are also good resources for assessing the qualifications for a particular role. While I acknowledge that job descriptions are sometimes written like online dating profiles, they are good indicators of what is needed to be successful in the role and the company. Looking at the job description and experience of people currently or previously in a specific role can help determine what experience you need to be competitive. Last, within personal and professional networks, there are tons of individuals who can provide an appraisal.

Learn to Lead

The homework phase requires you to be a continuous learner to remain current and competitive. Just like a home has a market value, so do people. Your market value increases by knowing and doing more. While you can try to tackle this process on your own, seeking out the assistance of others can be invaluable. Anyone who has achieved any level of success has had the assistance, guidance, feedback, or support of someone else. You just have to make the decision to ask for it. If the dream you selected requires you to be a leader, then you must be a continuous learner because the two are connected. The best way to become a continuous learner is to not fear making choices. When we choose, good or bad, we learn.

After reading this chapter and taking some time to reflect, I am now aware of:

The key ideas I wish to remember and share are:

STAGED!

I am going to apply what I have discovered by:

I am going to ask the following individual(s) to hold me accountable:

I will share my progress with them on (insert date):

Things to remember:

1) Be honest with yourself.

2) Ask for help in identifying and dealing with your blind spots.

3) Know your worth and what is required to achieve your dreams.

4) Be a continuous learner by not avoiding making choices.

5

DECLUTTER, CLEAN, REPAIR

God grant me the serenity to accept the things I cannot change;
courage to change the things I can; and wisdom to know the
difference.—Reinhold Niebuhr

Significance of Sequence (SOS)

As I mentioned earlier in the book, it is important to *be intentional*. I was very intentional with the order in which the words appear in the title for this chapter. I have come to learn that there is tremendous significance in sequence. In simplest terms, you must crawl before you walk and walk before you run. Whether you consider the job of an airline pilot or even of doctors in the emergency room, checklists are employed to make sure the proper sequence is followed to improve safety and reduce errors. Sequence should be given the same level of importance in your personal and professional life. When it comes to your career, business decisions, or even relationships, you should give careful consideration to the sequence in which you approach these things. So with that being said, the next home staging principle is to declutter.

Collectibles

When it comes to home staging, one of the biggest distractions is an overly cluttered home. What one may see as a collectible, someone else may view as clutter. The attachments people have to their stuff, which they live with every day, make seeing it as clutter difficult, while buyers will spot it immediately. This situation is similar to blind spots. Clutter eats up space, limiting the ability to grow or expand. Clutter is also connected to chaos, which breeds confusion. Distracted buyers don't see the home or see themselves in the home; all they see is the homeowner's stuff, which makes it difficult for them to make a decision. This is the reason for decluttering.

One could easily misinterpret the application of decluttering to mean getting rid of all evidence of who you are to create a false image. When you decide to purse your dreams, the role of your "belongings" change. They now need to support your goals. This is why it is important to eliminate anything that may distract or even be offensive to you or those who you wish to help make your dream a reality. Getting rid of things from the past that is taking up space makes room for the present and the future. It is important for you to always save room for opportunity, because it does not run on a set schedule. If opportunity is not predictable, what can be? *You!* You can be prepared for that moment when opportunity does knock. Decluttering is your opportunity to remove personal issues and attachments so that you can get to the next phase of the process, cleaning.

What clutter needs to be removed from your life in order for you to accomplish your goals or dreams?

Real World, Real Things Moments
Hoarding

Some of you may be fans of the TV show *Hoarders*. If you have seen the show, I'm sure during at least one episode, if not all of them, you had to look away from the TV. While the shocking images revealed the dark side of extreme compulsive hoarding, the comments from the cleanup specialist and psychologist highlight the fact that we all do a little hoarding in our own way. We hold on to negative things people may have done or said to us, we hold on to previous failures or disappointments, and we hold on to unsubstantiated ideas about ourselves. Many people with compulsive hoarding do not recognize how bad the problem really is; often, it is a family member who is most bothered by the clutter. This sounds very familiar to the discussion on blind spots and denial. We become some so used to living with these thoughts or experiences that we do not see the impact it is having on us and the people around us. What I first thought was laziness in hoarders, I now understand to be a mental disorder that makes it difficult to make choices and realize the impact it has on the individual and those around them. The most important lesson I learned from *Hoarders* is that there is a significant difference between making a sacrifice and making a choice.

What choices are you prepared to make to accomplish your goals or dreams?

I hope it is clear to you why I felt the need to introduce the concept of hoarding as we discuss decluttering. My goal was to not diagnose everyone as a hoarder, but I strongly believe we can all find examples of when we may have found ourselves having difficulty processing information, letting go of certain beliefs about our possessions, or experiencing emotional distress when forced to make a choice. What is also important to reinforce is that most hoarders required the assistance of a specialist. Hoarder or not, making decisions can be difficult, and sometimes you need the assistance of an expert.

Mr. Clean

After decluttering, the next staging principle is cleaning. Decluttering allows you to see what needs to be cleaned. By removing unnecessary items, there is also less stuff to clean, meaning cleaning will take less time. A clean house shows pride of ownership, makes people more comfortable, eliminates odors, and makes a home feel more spacious.

Real World, Real Things Moments
Flo's Cleaning Process

My mother always instructed me to clean from the top down and from the back of the house to front of the house. I did it because she instructed me to do it, but as I started writing this chapter it had a new meaning. When you start at the bottom, you run the risk of the stuff at the top falling back to bottom, thereby prolonging the process or introducing you to the concept of insanity. Cleaning from the back of the house helps you to not backtrack dirt into rooms that have already been cleaned.

Clean Slate

Start by doing what's necessary; then do what's possible; and suddenly you are doing the impossible."—St. Francis of Assisi

So what does this all mean? Once again, sequence is a critical component of achieving your goals in an efficient manner. While you may be willing to let go of certain things, you also have to be willing to clean up what's left in a way that doesn't allow the "dirt" to creep back into your life. Think back to the section on the sniff test and blind spots. How do you make sure that those issues identified in that process do not resurface? Having a plan, practicing, and being persistent are how you will start to develop good habits. It is not enough to just throw something away. You have to be willing to forgive and forget it so that you do not fall back into your old ways. Some people, ideas, and habits need a one-way ticket out of your life.

License. Please.

No matter how well a home is decluttered and cleaned, it will not sell if it needs serious repairs. Before a home can be sold, many states require a home inspection by a licensed home inspector. This individual will do a thorough inspection, which includes examining everything from the foundation to the roof. A home inspection looks at significant defects and safety considerations. The home inspection can then be used as a guide to address a home's major issues. While the homeowner can handle some issues, others that have been festering for years or that can lead to unintended consequences if not handled appropriately, should be managed by a specialist. Homeowners are often hesitant to spend money to fix up a home just to sell it. I am a strong believer in the idea that you either pay now or you end up paying later. Failure to make required repairs is a failure to adequately prepare, therefore preemptively limiting the potential of the home.

Buzz Kill

If a home is listed still needing repairs and it does not sell, the buzz factor is gone, which is difficult to regenerate. While cliché, it still holds true that you never get a second chance to make a first impression. A home can be ready for sale in a matter of weeks with proper planning, but it should not be rushed. Certain activities need to be tackled in a certain order (remember SOS) or the whole process may grind to a halt.

Real World, Real Things Moments
Personal Home Inspection

Find yourself a "home" inspector. This could be a mentor, career counselor, life coach, psychologist, headhunter, or even a friend. They can be extremely helpful in your quest to understand what needs to be fixed on a professional or personal level. Failure to make the necessary repairs means all the work you may have done to this point would have been in vain. One of the best things I've ever done for myself was speak to a counselor. While I had done a lot of work on my own, I really needed their expertise to understand why I felt the way I did, why I did the things I did, and how I could take the proper steps to make sure the beliefs I discarded, behaviors I cleaned up, and relationships I repaired, stayed that way. The counselor was also extremely helpful in pointing out how things from my personal life were impacting my beliefs and behavior in a professional setting. Do not let failure to ask for help limit your potential and kill your buzz.

A Room With A View

How many personal or professional opportunities might you have missed out on because you were not prepared? I am normally not one to dwell on the past, but sometimes looking backwards provides perspective, which allows you to move forward more confidently. Unless you are willing to continuously work on improving by taking an objective look at yourself and enlisting the support of others, you may find yourself in a pattern of missed opportunities. When was the last time you took inventory of what is most important to you? In a world of limited resources, where do you want to spend your time and energy? What if giving up some of your "stuff" gave you more time or energy to invest in your goals, your dreams, or even others? This part of the staging process is likely the most difficult because it deals with two issues that most people struggle with. Those two things are comfort and risk.

Depending on your personality, they can be equally enjoyable or equally scary. When was the last time you took a risk? Unless you take risks, you will not be stretched; you will not grow, and you will not gain. Once you have completed your homework, decluttered, cleaned, and made the required repairs on the inside, it is now time to step outside and check out the view from the curb.

After reading this chapter and taking some time to reflect, I am now aware of:

The key ideas I wish to remember and share are:

I am going to apply what I have discovered by:

I am going to ask the following individual(s) to hold me accountable:

I will share my progress with them on (insert date):

Things to remember:

1) There is significance in sequence.

2) When you decide to pursue a new goal or dream, the role of your past, the people in your life, and your personal belongings must change to support your new direction.

3) Because opportunity is unpredictable, you must always strive to be prepared.

4) Having a plan and executing it regularly is the key to building good habits.

5) Some repairs require the assistance of a specialist.

6

CURB APPEAL

Watts Up?

At a basic level, curb appeal is the overall impression the front of a home makes. Prospective buyers will formulate an opinion about the exterior of a home in the first fifteen seconds, and it will set their expectations for the interior. The view from the curb often determines whether a buyer will even consider giving a home a closer look, and any signs of neglect can instantly make them turn away. I always thought of curb appeal as simply landscaping. However, I have come to understand that it includes your sidewalk, roof, doors, windows, garage doors, doorbell, mailbox, and lighting. Of all of these items, it appears lighting is the star of curb appeal. Most staging resources emphasize high-wattage lightbulbs to make a home stand out. A lightbulb went off in my head—pun intended—that made me think about what wattage I would be if I were a lightbulb. How about you? Are you forty, sixty, or a hundred watts?

Shine Your Light

Hands down, one of my favorite songs growing up was "This Little Light of Mine." When I got to the part that said, "I'm going to let it shine," I made sure everyone knew how serious I was by singing louder than the choir. While growing up in the church, I remember hearing sermons where my pastor would quote Matthew 5:14, "You are the light of the world," or Matthew 5:16, "Let your light so shine before men, that they may see your good works." The Bible verses inform us that we all have light within us and we have a responsibility to use it so others may see the positive things we are doing. This is why the process requires you to share what you are learning with others; you never know the impact it may have on others. I also want to reemphasize the importance of using your light in your own way, without artificial or borrowed light. Your best self will always be your authentic self.

Real World, Real Things Moment
Drive By

My wife and I enjoy driving through neighborhoods we like at night to check out the homes for sale. If we like the way the exterior of the home looks at night, my wife will pull up the home on her real estate app to see the interior. Why am I telling you this, other than to let you know we have some weird hobbies? You never know who could drive by your "house" or what time of the day or night they will choose to do so; you never know when opportunity—a chance encounter with a potential employer, investor, or even partner—will arise, so you have to make sure you are always at your best. You want to be the home whose light is shining brightest on a dark street.

Snip

Needless to say, buyers are looking at everything when making up their minds about a home, and cutting corners will likely shortchange any return on investment. Shortcuts often shortchange results. This is why I have emphasized following a process and the significance of sequence. Things must be done properly, and in order. Let's say a homeowner focused on curb appeal, which may get someone's attention. If the interior is the complete opposite of the exterior, they may not get a second chance to make a good impression. Do not make the mistake of being all shine and no substance.

Who Am I?

So when you arrived at the chapter, Curb Appeal, how did you think this staging principle would apply to your personal or professional goals? Personal appearance? Being visible? Standing out, but fitting in? Knowing how others see you? If you answered yes to any of the above, you are correct. I would summarize these statements under the umbrella of personal branding. Before I go any further, I have to admit that "personal branding" has become an overused term and has drifted away from its original intent. Most of the focus of personal branding is on creating an image, managing your social media presence, and developing personal branding statements for resumes and interviews, among other topics. While personal branding does encompass all of these things, there was one thing I was looking for that I did not come across.

If you do not create your own personal brand, one will be created for you.

x

Trust Me!

A brand is a person's instinctual reaction to a product, service, or company. Our brains are wired to notice what's different, and our gut confirms our intuition. How do people see you? What makes you different? Why should people want to know you or listen to you? The foundation of a brand is trust. The foundation of a good relationship is also trust. Your personal brand is directly correlated to your relationship with people. People will trust your brand when their experience consistently meets or beats their expectations. Would you rather trust your brain and gut when assessing if someone is trustworthy, or take their word for it when they say, "You can trust me"?

Real World, Real Things Moment
Control

Having a personal brand created for you is not necessarily a bad thing. When I was in high school, my girlfriend gave me the nickname "The Total Package." Once I embraced it, I owned it. Funnily enough, for senior year superlatives, I was voted "Best All Around." However, not all personal brands follow the same path. We know people who are considered "shy," "drama queens," "pretentious," and "guarded" who would vehemently disagree that those words should be applied to them. This is another example of how blind spots shape people's perceptions of you. If you do not want to be at the complete mercy of people's perceptions, then it is up to you to control your personal brand and accept the responsibility that comes along with deciding to do so.

Super Natural vs. Supernatural

For some, proactively managing their brand requires hard work and dedication. It can become a burdensome task when they are not genuine in defining who they are and how their character plays out in the public. Your personal brand should be an honest representation of the values and habits that form the basis for your character. When you are being yourself, it is easier for people to know what they can expect during each encounter with you. Therefore, your brand should be something that comes naturally to you—it's instinctual. Some people confuse personal branding with "acting the part." It is okay to look up to someone as a role model and want to pattern yourself after them, but you have to make it your own.

What do you believe is your personal brand?

Who Am I To You?

If you are struggling to come up with an answer to this question, ask your close friends, co-workers, or family members. I recommend casting a broad net that covers different social environments to see where there are similarities and differences. Ask them, what words would they use to describe you? What is having a relationship with you like? You may hear things that you like or dislike. It is okay to reference the steps discussed about receiving feedback during this process as well. Sometimes the biggest ah-ha comes from the fact that people think more highly of you than you do of yourself. I also want to prepare you for the fact that you may hear very different things from each person you ask. If you do, it is okay. It can be extremely challenging to have your brand be the same to various individuals you interact with in different settings or to people who may have known you in different stages of your life. All I ask is that once you determine or identify your personal brand, you strive to be the same person in every encounter and setting. When you start to see yourself as a brand, your perspective will evolve and you will become more mindful about how you choose to live your life. You will learn to protect your brand while continuously molding and shaping it.

Real World, Real Things Moment
Shake it Up, Start Over

If you do not like your curb appeal, *change it. If you don't like your brand, re-brand yourself!* You will not be the first or the last person to hit the reset button on your brand. Consider the following individuals or companies who were able to bounce back from a bad situation or re-brand themselves: Bill Clinton, Robert Downey Jr., Britney Spears, Michael Vick, Mike Tyson, Chris Brown, Apple, Starbucks, Target, Wal-Mart, UPS, Old Spice, and Hyundai.

Toot It, But Don't Blow It!

Managing your brand is not solely about self-promotion. I would be lying if I didn't admit that it plays a part, but it is not the leading role. The staging principles and process was designed to help you uncover and understand your story so that when you share it with others, it will be obvious that it is not bragging but rather your way of providing them with a deeper understanding of who you truly are. The people who seem to be the happiest proclaim that it is because they get to be their authentic self, day in and day out and the rest just seems to take care of itself. When you have done your homework, decluttered, cleaned, made repairs, and worked on your curb appeal, it is then time to tell your story.

After reading this chapter and taking some time to reflect, I am now aware of:

The key ideas I wish to remember and share are:

I am going to apply what I have discovered by:

I am going to ask the following individual (s) to hold me accountable:

I will share my progress with them on (insert date):

Things to remember:

1) Do not try to dim your light. It is your competitive advantage.

2) You never know when opportunity will stop by, so make sure you have done what is needed so that it can find you.

3) If you do not create your own brand, one will be created for you.

4) Trust is the foundation of a good relationship with yourself and others.

5) Your authentic self is your best self.

1

TELL YOUR STORY

Say What?

We are entering the final stretch of the staging process. Staging involves more than just preparing the interior and exterior of the home. Maybe the most important part of the process is how you tell the story about the process and of the home. After speaking with several friends and family members who are realtors about what it takes to write a great real estate listing, they informed me that the keys are to be honest, be specific, provide motivation, and highlight unseen amenities. One comment was that omission is not considered an offense. While most people may think it is simple to write a real estate posting, it is actually quite difficult. So much so that there are actually companies that specialize in helping real estate agents and homeowners craft listings to give them the best shot of motivating a potential buyer to make an offer. I see significant overlap in what it takes write a compelling real estate listing and what is required to effectively tell your story. This last stage of the process underscores the importance of communication. In my opinion, impactful communication is predicated on being able to answer a few questions.

- Who is your audience?

- What are you saying?

- Why does it matter?

- How are you saying it?

To illustrate my point, I'll match two elements from a great real estate listing with two elements of good communication.

Real estate: providing motivation
vs.
Good communication: how you are saying it

Providing motivation addresses the question of how you are saying it. Great storytellers speak with passion. Passion is contagious and very motivating. People often question how I am able to infuse so much passion into my talks or presentations, and I always answer the same way: I just tell the truth, and it does all the work for me. If I truly believe in what I am saying, that will come across to my audience.

Real estate: highlighting unseen amenities
vs.
Good communication: why does it matter?

Highlighting unseen amenities ties in nicely to why it matters. This is your opportunity to point out what makes you different and why someone should listen to you and what you have to say. In other words, this is your moment to let people know what your competitive advantage is and how you stack up against the competition. A complementary point to this is the idea that omission is not a sin. This is not the same as saying you should lie, but there are certain things that are okay to keep to yourself or to share only with that person you trust unconditionally. My rationale for making this point is twofold. The first is

CONROD S. J. KELLY

that you cannot control how someone will react to the
information you will share and second, sometimes telling a
part of your story involves speaking about someone else in
a negative light. At the end of the day, the choice is yours.
Just make sure you are prepared to deal with all the
possible outcomes of sharing every detail of your story.

Fireside Chats

Words and ideas presented in a way that engages
listeners' emotions are what carry stories. It is this oral
tradition that lies at the center of our ability to motivate,
sell, inspire, and engage others. The beauty of storytelling
and its role in our traditions and history is the ability for it
to be re-told and passed along. Whether it is the story of
Christopher Columbus discovering America, or Paul
Revere warning that the redcoats are coming, or even
Humpty Dumpty falling off the wall, these stories have
endured over many generations. All those people who
have helped you along the way also know your story and
can tell it almost as well as you can. If they can't, it is your
responsibility to make sure that they can. Both you and
your "team" should be aware of all the quirks that make
you unique.

Real World, Real Things Moments
Sponsored By

If you read any book on climbing the corporate
ladder, there are three words you will likely come across:
mentors, coaches, and sponsors. While all three are
important, a sponsor is the individual that wields the most
power. Your sponsor knows your strengths and

weaknesses and is keenly aware of opportunities within and outside of your company. Sponsors can turn your dreams into realities. They connect, open doors, and sometimes even build doors. Most of the time you know exactly who they are, but sometimes they are unknown to you. Remember, someone is always watching. You should also be watching to see who inside or outside of your organization can help you achieve your goals, and you should always be prepared to let them know what you bring to the table to help boost their career, influence, or visibility. While some sponsors enjoy being sponsors, sometimes you just have to ask them to sponsor you and give them a compelling reason why they should. One of the most terrifying and proudest moments in my career was when I approached a vice president and told her that I wanted to be a part of her legacy.

Coming From Where I Am From

What I have come to learn is that the journey to become the best you, the real you, starts with understanding the story of your life. If you read the autobiographies of successful people, you discover a common theme of overcoming difficulties, tragedies, and failures. Your story may also stem from similar experiences or positive experiences. Positive or negative, your experiences should be used to bring meaning to your life. Your story provides the context for your experiences, and through it, you can find the inspiration to make an impact in the world. Telling your story is an opportunity to take people on a journey, a journey that allows them to connect with you in a deeper way or one that may inspire them to embark upon one of their own. Your story is a powerful engine and something that no one can take away from you. Having a strong intrinsic motivator is a competitive advantage. It is an eternal flame that can withstand any rain, wind, cold, or storm that may enter your life.

Once Upon A Time

So what does it take to be a good storyteller?

Purpose.

Passion.

Preparation.

Practice.

Great storytellers prepare obsessively. Their story is always a work in progress. They learn how to tell the short version, the long version, and the version that is audience-dependent. They practice so much that they can improvise on the drop of a dime. You too can be a great storyteller because you know the story inside and out. You have lived it your whole life. The process you have just gone through by reading this book could also make a great story. You have done your homework, decluttered, cleaned, repaired, improved your curb appeal and now the *stage* is *yours*. Tell your story!

You've been STAGED!

After reading this chapter and taking some time to reflect, I am now aware of:

The key ideas I wish to remember and share are:

I am going to apply what I have discovered by:

I am going to ask the following individual(s) to hold me accountable:

I will share my progress with them on:

Things to remember:

1) Your story is your competitive advantage. No one else has experienced your life but you.

2) Make sure you are not the only one who knows or can tell your story.

3) Your story is the seed that is rooted in your purpose.

8

THIS IS MY STORY

My reason for starting the book off with inception is because my story revolves around dreaming big. I put my goals and dreams into the universe, let other people know what I want, and then put a plan in place to pursue it. My pursuit involves preparing, practicing, and persisting, so that when the opportunity does come, I am ready to pounce on it. I have always been of the mindset that you have to ask for what you want. My best friend David introduced me to the concept of "what does it cost you to ask." For better or worse, this made me fearless. To keep me balanced, my mother introduced me to the concept of what God has for you—is for you. This statement taught me about patience and faith. I go into every situation confidently because I know that I have prepared, and if I do not get it, it was not meant for me to get it. God's timing is perfect. Don't believe me? Just watch.

Five for Five

If I had to choose five words to summarize my life story they would be faith, fearlessness, service, preparation, and persistence. From the time I entered this world, there were people building out dream worlds for me to fill with my own ideas, dreams, and goals. The first architect and extractor I met was my kindergarten teacher Mrs. Albury. She saw right through the quiet boy from Jamaica. She gave me more work, and harder work, than the other students in my class. I even spent the weekend at her home, putting together puzzles and playing word games. When she saw that I was able to get through all her assignments easily, she encouraged my mother to take me to get tested for the gifted program. The work she was giving me was to *prepare* me for the opportunity to have a private school education within the Dade County public school system.

The next extractor I encountered was Mrs. Horton, my fourth grade gifted teacher. She challenged me to not just be smart but to be mentally tough. She intentionally gave me assignments she knew I could not do to test my competitiveness and to introduce me to the concept of failure. I remember her dismissing the class for recess and giving me the option to go outside and play or keep working on the assignment. She wanted to see how long I would *persist* before giving up. What I first understood to be lessons in failure turned out to be an exercise in humility. She was the first to get me to utter the words "I don't know." Another one of her tricks was to switch me from the winning team to the losing team in the middle of a class competition to see if I would fight even harder to win. I learned from her how to bounce back from failure. I learned that there was opportunity in failure, because I could use what I learned from being on the winning team to help the struggling team. Maybe the most confusing and influential of her antics was calling our entire class names like nerds or geeks to desensitize us. She taught us not to shy away from our gifts or talents but to embrace them. When we started calling each other nerds and geeks in the hallway, the other students were shocked.

In the sixth grade I encountered an extractor by the name of Mrs. Hoffman. She was one of the toughest by far. She made me embrace the role of leader rather than fear it. She held me accountable for my actions because she saw the leadership potential I possessed. She taught me to be self-aware of how my actions influenced those around me. She also pushed me to set higher standards for myself. Mrs. Hoffman didn't let me off the hook for having good test grades, she also held me accountable for my behavior. She was the first to draw the connection between the two and how one could derail the other. Maybe the most important thing I learned from Mrs. Hoffman was the importance of being balanced by embracing my whole self. She allowed me to explore my creativity and embrace it as one of my strengths.

During this time, the most life-altering thing happened to me. I was chosen as peer mediator of the year for the state of Florida and selected to give a speech downtown at the Peer Mediator Conference. My mother's boss changed his mind about giving her the day off the day before the conference. In what I would call the most courageous act of *faith,* my mother quit her job so that she could see me give my speech. That was the first time I was introduced to faith. It is a moment I will never forget. I remember my mom telling me on the drive home that our steps had already been ordered and that everything was happening according to God's will. Could she have known then that that moment would change my life forever?

In the summer of my tenth-grade year I encountered Mrs. Josephine Stinson. Mrs. Stinson was the lead teacher for the Business and Finance Academy at a brand new magnet school named Coral Reef Senior High School. Because it was a new school, students were selected by a raffle process to be fair. Unfortunately, my name was not selected for the magnet I wanted to join. A few weeks later I got a call from Mrs. Stinson informing me that she had one spot left in her academy and that she had selected me from a list of hundreds of names because my name sounded like someone who was going to be famous. I guess that was pure luck.

Mrs. Stinson and I developed a good relationship, and I tried to repay her for her generosity by helping out in whatever way I could. Because I got to school so early, I would help make coffee and set up for her corporate advisory boards. She would also let me sit in on those meetings, which was a priceless experience. Early in my senior year, Florida A & M University was having a scholarship banquet and asked my principal to send four students. I was one of 435 seniors in my class, but Mrs. Stinson insisted that I be selected as one of the four from my school to attend the banquet. On the day of the banquet, everything that could go wrong did. Our ride was late, the skies opened up, and we even got lost. My mother prayed so hard that she almost crushed my hands. We got there just before the event was over and was immediately handed a paper to write down my GPA and SAT score. Ten minutes later, I was standing in the front of the room with the President of the university holding a full scholarship. The service I had provided to my school and lead teacher in addition to my preparation that resulted in high GPA and SAT scores afforded me a full ride for my undergraduate and Master's degree. What I walked away with from my experience on that day was the multiplier effect that service provides. From the time I was a child, my upbringing was rooted in the idea of hard work and service. I learned to lead by learning to serve. I received because I gave. I realized at a very early age that my purpose was service. When I am engaged in service, my energy is unlimited like the sun.

At the age of eighteen, I entered the School of Business and Industry at Florida A & M University. I committed to completing my MBA or walking away with nothing. This would require faith, fearlessness, persistence, and preparation. Excellence was the standard and nothing else was accepted. From eighteen years of age until the time I was twenty-three, I had the opportunity to sit face to face with countless CEOs and presidents from Fortune 500 companies. I also had the opportunity to be the CEO of one of the nineteen student-run companies that supported our business school. My university told us that we belonged and that we could compete with the best and the brightest because we would be the most prepared. They instilled fearlessness in us. The training I received there, along with all the lessons I had learned along the way, allowed me to received six six-figure job offers from Fortune 500 companies when I graduated. To this day, I have received an offer for every position that I have interviewed for. I want say that it was pure luck, but it all came down to preparation. I want every student or professional to be able to have a similar experience, and that is why I started STAGES, LLC.

My story is predicated on the fact that along the way, someone always believed in me. I've always carried that belief as a debt that I must repay. I have written this book because to whom much is given, much is expected. I was fortunate to have a team around me my whole life that wanted nothing more than to see me become a "superstar." I strongly believe that the difference between a star and a superstar is their team. I want to give you that same experience. That is why I have written this book to share my story and my process and also why I have started my company, STAGES. Through STAGES, everyone will have the opportunity to have the team required to make them a superstar.

Competitive Advantage

I am my competitive advantage.

My faith is my competitive advantage.

My fearlessness is my competitive advantage.

My persistence is my competitive advantage.

My preparation is my competitive advantage.

My passion is my competitive advantage.

My purpose is my competitive advantage.

My service is my competitive advantage.

My journey is my competitive advantage.

My voice is my competitive advantage

My story is my competitive advantage.

Our deepest fear is not that we are inadequate. Our deepest fear is that we are powerful beyond measure. It is our light, not our darkness, that most frighten us. We ask ourselves, who am I to be brilliant, gorgeous, talented, fabulous? Actually, who are you not to be? You are a child of God. Your playing small doesn't serve the world. There is nothing enlightened about shrinking so that other people won't feel insecure around you. We are all meant to shine, as children do. We were born to make manifest the glory of God that is within us. It's not just in some of us; it's in everyone. And as we let our own light shine, we unconsciously give other people permission to do the same. As we're liberated from our own fear, our presence automatically liberates others.

—Marianne Williamson

ABOUT THE AUTHOR

Conrod is the founder and CEO of STAGES, a career development company he started to help individuals on a larger scale after years of one-on-one career coaching. STAGED! describes the values and philosophy of the founder and company. Conrod draws on over ten years of experience at companies such as Johnson & Johnson, GlaxoSmithKline, and Merck—along with his many years as a student of personal and professional development to motivate and inspire others. Conrod is originally from Kingston, Jamaica, and grew up in South Florida. Conrod and his wife Joy reside in the Greater Philadelphia area.